JENNY'S PRAYER

To Alex and Kayla, the answer to my prayers, and
to Detlef for his faith in me
— A.G.

To my children, Casey, Christopher, and Elliot, who
have inspired so much of my art, and to Jim for his
great encouragement
— M.A.L.

Text Copyright © 1998 by Annette Griessman

Illustrations Copyright © 1998 by Mary Anne Lard

Morehouse Publishing
P.O. Box 1321
Harrisburg, PA 17105

Morehouse Publishing is a division of The Morehouse Group.

Printed in Malaysia

Cover design by Dana Jackson

Library-of-Congress Cataloging-in-Publication Data

Griessman, Annette.
    Jenny's Prayer / text by Annette Giessman ; illustrated by Mary Anne Lard.
        p.   cm.
        Summary: Jenny wants a kitten from a pet store but when she doesn't receive it after saying a prayer, she questions whether God is listening.
        ISBN 0–8192–1746–8 (hardcover)
        [1. Prayer—Fiction. 2. Cats—Fiction. 3. Pets—Fiction. 4. Christian Life—Fiction.] I. Lard, Mary, Anne, ill. II. Title.
PZ7.G881235Je   1998
[E]—dc21   98-21494
                                                              CIP
                                                              AC

Jenny's Prayer

Text by
Annette Griessman

Illustrated by
Mary Anne Lard

Jenny wanted the white kitten the moment she saw it prancing daintily around its carpeted cage. Its long, silky fur floated around its sky blue eyes. Its plump little belly wiggled as it pounced on an imaginary mouse. It was the loveliest kitten she had ever seen. Catching sight of her mother walking down the aisle with a large bag of bird seed in hand, Jenny jumped up, running after her.

Mom… Mom," she said, tugging at her mom's sleeve. "I've found the kitten I want! She's beautiful! Come look at her," she pleaded.

Jenny's mom looked at her watch as she paid the cashier. "Not today, dear," she said, putting the change in her purse and grabbing the shopping bag. "We're going to be late picking up your brother."

"But, Mom… you promised!" Mom didn't answer, but hurried from the store. Jenny darted after her, looking back to catch one last glimpse of white fur before the pet shop door closed. Jenny's heart sank as she got into the car. She had wanted a kitten ever since she could remember, and her Mom had told her she could have one when they found just the right one. That pretty kitten was perfect. Her mom hadn't even listened to her.

Later that evening, Jenny sat with her dad on the porch as he read the newspaper. "Dad?" she asked.

"Uh-huh," he muttered, not looking up from his paper.

Jenny told him about the kitten.

"A kitten? I'm afraid you'll have to talk to your mother, Jenny." He turned a page and continued reading.

"But Mom didn't listen!" cried Jenny.

Dad didn't answer, caught up in his news story.

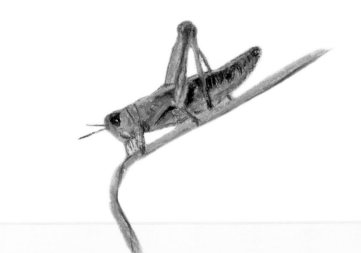

Jenny turned away. *And neither did you,* she thought sadly. She wandered out into the yard and sat under the shade of her favorite tree. Her thinking tree. Snuggling up next to the great, knobby trunk, she put her arms around her knees. She thought of the kitten—the way its blue eyes glistened and its fur puffed out like cotton candy. She wanted that kitten more than anything. And nobody seemed to care.

No, that wasn't true. Jenny knew of someone who would listen. She screwed her eyes shut and bowed her head. "Dear God, I'm sure you know I want that kitten from the pet store, since you know everything. Please help me get it, okay? I'll take real good care of it. I promise. Amen."

Jenny looked up, her eyes gleaming. Now she would get that kitten for sure! All she had to do was to get her mom to take her back to the pet store. She could almost feel the warm bundle of fluff in her arms.

She jumped up excitedly and ran inside to work on her mom. And this time she wouldn't give up until her mother listened.

Jenny's mom did listen, and the next morning as the car drove into the pet shop parking lot, Jenny bounced in her seat with excitement. Her mother remembered the promise she had made to Jenny, and now she had the time to look at the kitten.

When the car stopped, Jenny bounded out ahead of her mom, racing out of the bright sunshine and into the store. She darted around fish tanks and bird cages toward the carpeted cage in the back, her heart nearly bursting.

But when she finally reached it, her heart sank. The cage was empty. The little white kitten was gone.

Jenny's eyes filled with tears. She felt her mother's hand on her shoulder, but barely heard her words of comfort as she steered Jenny out of the store. All Jenny could think about was her prayer from the night before. She couldn't believe it. Even God hadn't listened to her.

That afternoon, Jenny sat on the back steps and watched her neighbor, Mrs. Jenkins, hang up her laundry on her clothesline. The gleaming white sheets snapped in the breeze but were quickly tamed by Mrs. Jenkins' quick hands and large supply of clothespins.

As Mrs. Jenkins worked, she noticed the quiet girl on the steps. She waved a hand, beckoning.

"Come on over, Jenny! I could use the company," she called.

Even though Jenny didn't feel like talking, she stood up
and shuffled over. She and Mrs. Jenkins visited often.
Jenny helped her in the summer with her garden. She loved
her like a grandmother.

Mrs. Jenkins frowned at Jenny's gloomy face. "It sure
looks like rain clouds are covering that sunny face of yours,"

she said, pulling another sheet from her basket. "What seems to be the trouble?"

In spite of herself, Jenny felt the corners of her mouth twitch. Mrs. Jenkins could always make her smile. She sat on the cool grass and told her about the white kitten and about nobody listening—not even God.

Mrs. Jenkins' forehead wrinkled and the corners of her mouth turned down. But her eyes were sure and calm as she turned toward Jenny, her sheets forgotten.

"Do you really believe that, Jenny?" she asked, her face intent.

Jenny shrugged, still filled with disappointment over the kitten.

"Yes," she answered simply. "If God had listened, I would have gotten that kitten."

Mrs. Jenkins cocked her head to the side with a strange smile. "Would you, now? Maybe God had other plans for that kitten." She leaned closer and lowered her voice. "Maybe He has other plans for you." She put her softly wrinkled hands on Jenny's shoulders, and her kind brown eyes locked with Jenny's own eyes. "But you can be sure, Jenny—God always listens."

For a moment, Jenny stood still. She saw the sureness of Mrs. Jenkins' belief in her eyes, but Jenny herself wasn't so sure that God always listens. She had wanted that kitten! She pulled away from Mrs. Jenkins' grasp and ran. She didn't stop until she was safely under the shelter of her thinking tree.

God didn't listen! she thought angrily. Mrs. Jenkins was wrong. Filled with angry thoughts, she leaned against the tree.

It was then that she saw two golden eyes looking at her from under a juniper bush.

Jenny held her breath. She timidly held out a hand. A small black body crawled hesitantly out of the shadows, blinking its large yellow eyes and sniffing. It crept up to Jenny's hand, touching it with a small, black nose. The kitten regarded Jenny silently for a moment, and then climbed into her waiting lap with a squeaky little meow.

Jenny petted the kitten in amazement. It wasn't silky and soft like the one in the pet shop. This one's fur was short and dirty, matted into clumps in places. It wasn't plump and dainty, either. Jenny could feel ribs move under its skin as it pushed its head hard against her, its whole body vibrating as it purred. But she was sure of one thing—unlike the kitten in the store, this kitten needed her as much as she needed it.

Jenny's heart filled with joy as she ran toward the house.

After a bath and a bowl of milk, the black kitten snuggled into Jenny's lap, full of contentment, and fell asleep. Jenny's mom smiled, watching her daughter and the kitten.

"Well, I guess you got your kitten after all," she said, putting the kitten's empty milk bowl into the sink.

Jenny nodded.

"He needs a name. Have you thought of what you're going to call him?"

Jenny looked at the kitten in her lap. He purred even as he slept. Jenny knew that the white kitten in the pet store hadn't been the one for her after all. She thought about what Mrs. Jenkins had said about God's plan for her. She smiled. "I'm going to call him Listens," she said.

Her mom gave her a curious look. "That's a funny name for a cat, isn't it?"

Jenny stroked the now-smooth fur with gentle fingers as she replied, "No, it's perfect."

Listens rolled over and gave a happy sigh.